19.15

DATE DUE

Sir Ernest Shackleton
and the Struggle Against Antarctica

Sir Ernest Shackleton
and the Struggle Against Antarctica

Hal Marcovitz

Chelsea House Publishers
Philadelphia

Prepared for Chelsea House Publishers by:
OTTN Publishing, Stockton, N.J.

CHELSEA HOUSE PUBLISHERS
Editor in Chief: Sally Cheney
Associate Editor in Chief: Kim Shinners
Production Manager: Pamela Loos
Art Director: Sara Davis
Director of Photography: Judy L. Hasday
Project Editors: LeeAnne Gelletly, Brian Baughan
Series Designer: Keith Trego

First Printing
1 3 5 7 9 8 6 4 2

Library of Congress Cataloging-in-Publication Data

Marcovitz, Hal.
    Sir Ernest Shackleton and the struggle against
    Antarctica / Hal Marcovitz.
        p. cm.–(Explorers of new worlds)
Includes bibliographical references and index.
ISBN 0-7910-6424-7 (alk. paper)
1. Shackleton, Ernest Henry, Sir, 1874-1922. 2. Explorers–Great Britain–Biography. 3. Antarctica–Discovery
and exploration. I. Title. II. Series.

G875.S5 M37 2001
919.8'904–dc21

                                    2001028300

Contents

Aboard the
James Caird

Large chunks of ice drift through the frigid waters of Antarctica. In 1916, Ernest Shackleton and five other men sailed an open boat nearly 2,000 miles through these dangerous waters, in order to get help for the stranded members of their expedition.

I

*T*he men aboard the 22-foot wooden lifeboat *James Caird* had spent 15 days dodging **icebergs** and braving the frigid Antarctic nights. But they knew they were close to land, because they had observed seabirds sitting on drifting masses of seaweed.

They were trying to make it to South Georgia, an island about 2,000 miles north of Antarctica toward South America. They knew they could find shelter there at a whaling station maintained by Norwegians. The men, under the command of the explorer Ernest Shackleton, were part of a larger party forced to abandon their ship when it was trapped and smashed by shifting ice floes off the Antarctic continent. Shackleton was determined to make it to South Georgia. He was responsible not only for the five other men in the *James Caird,* but also for the 22 members of their **expedition** left behind on a tiny island in the frigid Weddell Sea. Their only hope of rescue depended on the success of the *James Caird*'s voyage.

At first, the sailing aboard the *James Caird* had been smooth. During the first few days, they managed to cover 60 or 70 miles a day. Soon, though, the waves became choppy. With no shelter aboard the open lifeboat, the men had no protection from the freezing spray of the waves. It was impossible to stay dry.

On the fourth day, the group ran into a storm. The winds were blowing out from the continent, which meant the temperatures dipped below zero. As the spray from the waves froze on the boat, the men were forced to chip off the heavy ice to keep their small craft from sinking. The storm lasted until the sixth day. With clear skies, the men were able to calculate their position according to the sun's position in the sky. Miraculously, they were still on course, about 380 miles from South Georgia.

"We reveled in the warmth of the sun that day," Shackleton later wrote in his book *South!* "Life was not so bad, after all. We felt we were well on our way. Our gear was drying, and we could have a hot meal in comparative comfort."

The calm weather remained with them until the 11th day, and then the clouds returned. At midnight on May 5, 1916, Shackleton was at the **tiller** of the *James Caird* when he thought he saw the sky clearing ahead. Then he realized that he was not looking at a clear sky, but at a tremendous wave approaching the *James Caird.* It was so broad that it completely filled the horizon.

"I realized that what I had seen was not a rift in the clouds but the white crest of an enormous wave," Shackleton wrote. "During twenty-six years' experience of the ocean in all its moods I had not encountered a wave so gigantic. It was a mighty upheaval of the ocean, a thing quite apart from the big white-capped seas that had been our tireless enemies for days. I shouted, 'For God's sake, hold on! It's got us!'"

The wave crashed into the tiny boat. The men held on, then started bailing frantically, using whatever they could grab to throw the seawater back overboard. Somehow, Shackleton and the others managed to keep the *James Caird* from **capsizing**.

The next day, the skies cleared. The explorers calculated that they were now 100 miles from South Georgia. But as night fell on the 15th day of their journey, a storm started blowing toward the *James Caird.* Shackleton feared that all would be lost.

Luckily, the fierce Antarctic weather spared the men. "Just when things looked their worst, they changed for the best," Shackleton would later write. "I have marveled often at the thin line that divides success from failure and the sudden turn that leads from apparently certain disaster to comparative safety. The wind suddenly shifted, and we were free once more."

They had escaped the storm, but they still had to endure one final night aboard the *James Caird.* Their big enemy now was their thirst. The drinking water aboard the lifeboat had run out some days before, and seawater, which is saturated with salt, is not **potable**. The men were dehydrated and weary— sleep aboard the tiny lifeboat had been almost impossible. "The pangs of thirst attacked us with redoubled intensity, and I felt that we must make a landing on the following day at almost any hazard," wrote Shackleton. "The night wore on. We were very tired. We longed for day. When at last the dawn came on the morning of May 10 there was practically no wind, but a high sea was running. We made slow progress to the shore."

By eight o'clock in the morning, Shackleton had spotted a strip of shore he recognized as King Haakon Bay in South Georgia. Shackleton decided to make a landing along the

This magazine illustration from the early 1900s shows Shackleton in the warm clothes he wore during his attempts to conquer Antarctica.

rocky shore of the bay. Soon, the wind started blowing out toward the tiny boat. The men rowed hard, fighting both the wind and the tide. For four hours they strained, looking for a passageway through the *reefs* that guarded the shore. If the *James Caird* struck a reef, the small boat would surely break apart. Making matters worse, the search for a safe place to land had taken hours, and now night was approaching again. If Shackleton failed to steer the *James Caird* through the reefs, the men would have to spend another night aboard the lifeboat. With no water and the men near exhaustion, Shackleton knew another night in the elements would surely mean the deaths of all hands.

Suddenly, Shackleton spotted a gap in the reefs. Beyond the gap he saw a stretch of clear shore and smooth water. The men bore down and shot through the gap. The waves pushed the lifeboat onto the beach, and Shackleton jumped ashore. He held tightly to a rope to keep the boat close to the beach while a wave rolled in. When the water became stable again, the other five men aboard the *James Caird*

> "The entrance [gap in the reef] was so narrow that we had to take in the oars," Shackleton wrote, "but in a minute or two we were inside, and in the gathering darkness the *James Caird* ran in on a swell and touched the beach."

jumped ashore as well. Shackleton tied the rope around a rock to anchor the lifeboat.

Shackleton later wrote:

> In a few minutes we were all safe on the beach, with the boat floating in the surging water just off the shore. We heard a gurgling sound that was sweet music to our ears, and, peering around, found a stream of fresh water almost at our feet. A moment later, we were down on our knees drinking the pure, ice-cold water in long draughts that put new life into us. It was a splendid moment.

The landing had saved the voyage. However, Shackleton and his men were hardly out of danger. The Norwegian whaling station was on the other side of South Georgia. A 17-mile hike over an unforgiving icy mountain range was still ahead of them.

A painting of Ernest Shackleton, from the collection of the Royal Geographic Society. As a young sailor, Shackleton became fascinated with the icy lands to the south, and hoped one day to explore Antarctica.

The Mysterious South

2

$\mathcal{E}$rnest Henry Shackleton was born on February 15, 1874, in County Kildare, Ireland. Ernest's parents, Henry and Henrietta Shackleton, were well-to-do landowners. However, when Ernest was young, his father decided to give up farming and start a new career in medicine. He attended Trinity College in Dublin and by 1884 had his degree in medicine. He moved his family to England and opened a practice just outside of London.

In 1887, Shackleton left home to attend Dulwich College, a school in London. Henry Shackleton hoped his son would follow him into medicine, but Ernest had other ideas. He left Dulwich after three years to join the crew of the *Hoghton Tower*, a sailing ship with tall masts and billowing sails. He was only 16 years old.

The *Hoghton Tower* was owned by the North Western Shipping Company, and it sailed out of Liverpool, a port city on England's western shore. Shackleton's first experience at sea was quite exciting. Heading for Valparaíso on the coast of the South American country of Chile, the *Hoghton Tower* ran into rough weather while rounding Cape Horn on the southernmost tip of South America. The crew of the *Hoghton Tower* battled storms for nearly two months before finding calm waters. The trip home was just as hazardous–the ship made it back to Liverpool just as the crew's food and water ran out.

Nevertheless, this was Ernest Shackleton's first taste of adventure, and he ached for more. Years later, after he had made his mark as an explorer, Shackleton told a newspaper reporter that his experiences aboard the *Hoghton Tower* and other ships convinced him to devote his future to exploring the far reaches of the globe.

"I think it came to me during my first voyage," Shackleton told the journalist. "I felt strangely drawn towards the mysterious south. We rounded

A clipper sails through ice around Cape Horn in this 19th-century illustration. Shackleton later said this portion of his first sea voyage, aboard the Hoghton Tower, *inspired him to explore the Antarctic.*

Cape Horn in the depth of winter. It was one continuous blizzard all the way. Yet many a time, even in the midst of all this discomfort, my thoughts would go out to the southward. But strangely enough, the circumstances which actually determined me to become an explorer was a dream I had when I was twenty-two. We were beating out to New York from Gibraltar, and I dreamt I was standing on the bridge in mid-Atlantic and looking northward. It was a simple dream. I seemed to vow to myself that some day I would go to the region of ice and snow and go on until I came to one of the poles of the Earth, the end of the *axis* upon which this great ball turns."

❧❧❧❧❧❧

Antarctica is one of Earth's seven continents, and the only one without a native human population. On the other six continents–North America, South America, Europe, Asia, Africa, and Australia–human habitation dates back tens of thousands of years. In Antarctica, however, the first humans set foot on the continent just over a hundred years ago.

It is easy to see why. The terribly cold temperatures and lack of food make it impossible for humans and most other living things to make their homes on Antarctica. Even today, the continent is home to only a handful of scientific outposts and some hardy penguins, although the seas around the continent contain abundant marine life.

Why is the climate so cold in Antarctica? Because the Earth is round and spins on its axis, polar regions lose more of the sun's heat to space than do regions at the center of the planet. The warm air at the center rises into the atmosphere, cooling as it approaches the poles. This cooler air then flows back toward the *equator*. It blows out of Antarctica, as well as the Arctic Circle, in the form of dry, icy winds.

And so Antarctica is forever frozen. Even on the warmest days, the average temperature is –5 degrees Fahrenheit. During winter, temperatures average –50 degrees, although temperatures as cold as 127 degrees below zero have been recorded on the continent.

The continent itself is generally circular in shape. The Transantarctic Mountains border the Pacific Ocean side of the continent in West Antarctica. Also on the western side is the Ross Sea, which cuts into the continent, although much of the sea is under ice. On the opposite side, a finger of land known as the Antarctic *Peninsula* juts out into the Atlantic Ocean. Bordering the peninsula is the Weddell Sea. There are few other

Antarctica is considered a land mass because underneath all its ice is a rocky core. In fact, a mountain range crosses the continent, and it is believed that the mountains contain deposits of coal. On the other hand, the Arctic Circle, at the top of the world, is a mass of frozen water. If it all melted, there would be no land underneath.

The Weddell Sea cuts into an ice shelf. Because of its location, it is always winter in Antarctica—the average temperatures range from -5 degrees to -50 degrees Fahrenheit.

natural features found in Antarctica. It's mostly ice— 5.5 million square miles of it.

Because of the tilt of the Earth, the continent experiences daylight that lasts anywhere from a few hours in winter to a full six months when Antarctica is pointed directly toward the sun.

Finally, the South Pole is located in Antarctica. The South Pole and the North Pole at the northern-most tip of the world are the hubs of the axis around which the planet spins.

Although the Antarctic waters were visited as early as 1774 by the English explorer James Cook, the first humans to set foot on Antarctica were men under the leadership of Norwegian Karsten Borchgrevink, who arrived on February 18, 1899. The expedition landed at Cape Adare on the western end of the Ross Sea. They didn't get very far inland. Borchgrevink and his men spent nearly a year at Cape Adare, carrying out occasional treks over the ice and charting the weather. Later, they explored several Antarctic islands.

By the early 1900s, the idea of exploring the inland of the continent—and locating the South Pole—had caught the attention of several of the era's bold explorers. In 1901, two expeditions made their way to Antarctica. The first was led by German Erich von Drygalski. His ship arrived in Antarctica in January 1902, but the vessel became locked in ice and was unable to continue. Drygalski carried out some explorations by dog sled. In February 1903, the ice shifted and Drygalski's ship was able to break out and return north.

The other expedition was led by a man who would have a great influence on the life of Ernest Shackleton—Robert Falcon Scott.

"I don't hold that anyone but an Englishman should get to the S[outh] Pole," explorer Robert Falcon Scott wrote in 1909. A veteran of the British Navy, Scott would become one of the most famous Antarctic explorers.

March Across the Ice

3

*E*nglishman Robert Falcon Scott first went to sea at the age of 13. In 1887, when Scott was 18 and serving as a midshipman aboard the Royal Navy ship *Rover*, he and four other midshipmen raced small sailboats across the bay of the Caribbean island St. Kitts. Scott won the race, and as a reward was invited to supper by the *Rover's* captain, Albert Markham. Also joining Scott and the captain for dinner that night was the captain's cousin, Clements Markham, a geographer and writer. Clements Markham was so impressed with Scott's enthusiasm and intensity that he would later write, "My final conclusion was that Scott was the destined man to command the Antarctic expedition."

Scott spent the next 14 years steadily rising in rank. In the meantime, his old friend Clements Markham had attained power and influence in the Royal Geographic Society. In 1894, the society began making plans to finance an Antarctic exploration. It took Markham six years of tireless work, but in 1900 he announced that the Royal Geographic Society had raised the money it needed to outfit an exploration to search for the South Pole. Markham, who had kept track of Scott's career, asked the Royal Navy to release Scott from service so that he could command the expedition. Scott began preparing for the voyage.

At the same time, Ernest Shackleton was climbing the ranks in the **merchant marine**. After his experience aboard the *Hoghton Tower*, Shackleton spent five years sailing in the merchant fleet. He quickly rose in rank. By 1898, the 24-year-old was certified to captain a merchant ship.

In the meantime, Shackleton met Emily Dorman, a friend of his sister. To be nearer to Emily, Shackleton took a job on the Union Castle Line, which mostly made mail and cargo runs between

England and South Africa. His new job required Shackleton to be gone no more than two months at a time, instead of the year-long voyages he had been making for much of his career at sea.

In the summer of 1900, Shackleton was in London when he heard that Scott would be heading an expedition to the Antarctic with the goal of finding the South Pole. Shackleton applied for a position in Scott's party, but was at first turned down. Shackleton then asked for help from some friends in the Royal Geographic Society. They arranged for him to meet with Albert Armitage, the navigator and Scott's second-in-command.

As a Union Castle ship captain, Shackleton helped transport British troops to South Africa to participate in the Boer War (1899-1902). The Boers were descended from the region's original Dutch settlers, and they were fighting to prevent the British from gaining control of the mineral-rich country.

Shackleton impressed Armitage, and the navigator urged Scott to find a place for the young man. Of Shackleton, Armitage later wrote: "His brother officers considered him a very good fellow, always quoting poetry and full of erratic ideas."

Scott agreed to find him a place aboard his ship, the *Discovery*. He named Shackleton third lieutenant in charge of provisions and deep sea water analysis.

The *Discovery* sailed on August 6, 1901. On January 8, 1902, the ship was making its way around the huge Antarctic icebergs when the crew sighted land. The *Discovery* cruised along the coastline for a number of weeks. During the voyage, Scott and Shackleton were lifted aloft in a hot-air balloon that was tethered to the deck of the *Discovery,* enabling the explorers to have an aerial view of the landscape. But the balloon developed a leak and was never used again. Finally, the *Discovery* anchored in McMurdo Sound, a stretch of Antarctic coastline along the Ross Sea.

During the next two years, members of the Scott expedition would make significant discoveries. For example, they found Taylor Valley, a remarkable region that is largely free of ice and snow. They also traveled to the east of McMurdo Sound and explored an area of the Antarctic coastline, which they named the Edward VII Peninsula, in honor of the king of England.

They performed several scientific experiments, including tracking the weather, gathering rocks where they could find them, and taking samples of the sparse plant life they found in Antarctica. Mostly they found lichens, mosses, and algae–small, non-leafy plants that require little water and sunlight and can survive the harshest weather conditions.

They also performed experiments to measure the *magnetism* in Antarctica. The earth's magnetism is a powerful force that attracts iron objects. This is caused by the planet's rotation, which creates a strong magnetic field near the North and South Poles. Compass needles are attracted to the magnetism of these poles. This was extremely important to explorers, because the compass was one of the best navigation tools they had. Therefore, Scott's party—and Antarctic missions that would follow–spent a lot of time studying the magnetic forces on the continent.

While Scott and his men spent a lot of time exploring

Because the Earth is tilted slightly, the North and South Poles aren't exactly in line with the magnetic poles of the Earth. In fact, the South Pole–the southernmost point of the earth–is about 1,600 miles from the magnetic south pole, which is actually in the Pacific Ocean, just off the coast of Antarctica.

Clothing and equipment used by the members of Scott's 1901-04 expedition. The goggles at the lower right were used to prevent snow blindness, a painful condition caused by sunlight reflected off snow and ice.

the nearby terrain and conducting scientific experiments, the goal of the mission was to find the South

Pole. On November 2, 1902, Scott, Shackleton, and the expedition's physician, Dr. Edward Adrian Wilson, left the camp at McMurdo Sound and headed due south in search of the South Pole. They were traveling by dog sled. A second party, under the command of Lieutenant Michael Barne, set out as well. The going was slow. On the third day out, a blizzard swept through eastern Antarctica and the teams were forced to take shelter in their tents. While waiting out the blizzard, Shackleton developed a cough.

When the blizzard passed, the mission continued. The explorers soon entered a vast plain. By mid-November, they had reached the 79th parallel of *latitude*. At this point, they were still about 1,000 miles from the South Pole. Barne's team decided to turn back, but Scott elected to continue.

Things would go badly for Scott's team. Unknown to the explorers, the food they had brought for the dogs had spoiled on board the *Discovery*. The dogs refused to eat the food, and as the trek continued the animals grew weak and many died. To feed the surviving dogs, the men butchered the corpses of the dead dogs for meat.

On November 25, Scott and his men crossed the

80th parallel. "We cannot stop, we cannot go back and there is no alternative but to harden our hearts and drive," Scott wrote. "The events of the day's march are now becoming so dreary and dispiriting that one longs to forget them when we camp; it is an effort even to record them in a diary. Our utmost efforts could not produce more than three miles for the whole march."

Shackleton's cough had grown worse during the march across the ice. Now his gums were swollen. Dr. Wilson was also battling illness. On December 26, *snow blindness* was making it almost impossible for the doctor to see. A day later, he had to march blindfolded as Shackleton and Scott directed him step by step.

All three men were hungry. Provisions were running low, so the men had to endure the trek with very little food. "Hunger is gripping us very tightly," wrote Scott.

On December 31, they reached the base of a 3,000-foot mountain that Scott named Mount Albert Markham, in honor of Scott's old captain aboard the *Rover*. They had reached the 82nd parallel, 480 miles from the South Pole—closer than anyone had yet been. Scott decided to turn for home.

Edward A. Wilson, the doctor on Scott's 1901 expedition, painted this scene of the men hauling their supplies across the Great Ice Barrier. On the trip back to the Discovery, *the dogs were too weak to pull the sleds.*

The trip back to the base at McMurdo Sound would prove just as treacherous. The dogs continued to die. By now, the remaining ones were so weak that Scott, Shackleton, and Wilson cut them free from the sleds and hauled the loads themselves while the dogs followed behind.

On January 18, 1903, Shackleton was so ill that Scott had to stop the march so Shackleton could rest. Shackleton had developed *scurvy*, a disease brought on by a lack of vitamin C in his diet. Vitamin C is found in fruits and vegetables–foods that were in short supply to the explorers. Shackleton's throat was congested, his breathing labored, his gums swollen, and he was coughing up blood.

After resting, the men continued their trek across the ice. Finally, on February 3, they arrived back in camp. Scott, Shackleton, and Wilson had been gone 93 days. They had marched across nearly 1,000 miles of the frozen Antarctic terrain.

Shackleton wanted to remain in Antarctica because Scott was considering another attempt to reach the South Pole. However, after Shackleton and the others left, Scott decided he was not ready to make another run for the Pole. He returned to England in April 1904.

When they returned, they found a second ship, the *Morning*, had arrived at McMurdo Sound. It carried much-needed supplies.

Eight members of the expedition decided to return to England aboard the *Morning*. Shackleton wanted to stay. His health had greatly improved in the weeks since the trek to the Pole had ended. However, Scott insisted that he leave with the others. In his diary, Scott wrote about Shackleton: "On board he would have remained a source of anxiety, and would never have been able to do hard out-door work."

On March 2, 1903, the *Morning* set sail with Shackleton aboard. Albert Armitage, Scott's navigator, also returned on the *Morning*. Later, Armitage would write that on the voyage home Shackleton promised to return to Antarctica, and that he had resolved to beat Scott to the South Pole. Shackleton, Armitage wrote, intended to "prove that he was a better man than Scott."

"I Cannot
Think of
Failure"

A painting of Shackleton's ship, the Nimrod, *in icy McMurdo Sound, near the explorer's eventual winter camp. During this 1907-08 journey, Shackleton came closer to the South Pole than any previous explorer.*

4

Shackleton would have to wait five years for his next Antarctic mission. In the meantime, he found a job as a journalist, then joined the Royal Geographic Society himself and rose in rank to secretary. Now, he enjoyed a position of influence in the organization that financed many of England's voyages of discovery.

He also married Emily on April 9, 1904. "I am so happy, dearest, thinking about all the times which are to be in our future," he wrote to her. "We do want to settle down and have our own house at last after all these years of waiting."

In 1907, Shackleton was approached by the Royal Geographic Society to head a mission to Antarctica. The South Pole still had not been reached. Shackleton quickly agreed and started making plans for the adventure.

The expedition left England in June 1907 aboard the ship *Nimrod*, arriving in New Zealand on November 23, 1907. It stayed in the harbor in New Zealand until January 1, 1908, then cast off its lines and sailed for Antarctica. To save fuel, the tugboat *Koonya* was enlisted to tow the *Nimrod* as far south as the Antarctic Circle, just before the 70th parallel.

Shackleton decided that the *Nimrod* would make its way to Antarctica, deposit the men and supplies on the continent, then return to New Zealand before the ship became stuck in ice. Once in Antarctica, Shackleton and his men would make camp for the winter. When spring arrived, the expedition would split into three teams. Two teams would explore the Antarctic coastlines while the third team would make a run for the Pole.

The most important cargo aboard the *Nimrod*

was the hut that would shelter the men against the harsh Antarctic weather. It was made of fir timbers, reinforced with iron cleats, bolts, and rods. The walls and roof were covered with thick felt and ground-up cork to provide ***insulation*** against the cold. Once in Antarctica, the hut was fastened to the ground by wooden timbers and steel cables, so it could resist the strong Antarctic winds.

Shackleton had signed up 11 men to serve in the expedition. They included men with backgrounds in meteorology, geology, biology, photography, medicine, and mapmaking. Also, he brought along a cook, an electrician, and other crew members who would look after the equipment and animals.

Shackleton had a clear idea of what he expected from his crew:

> The personnel of an expedition of the character I proposed is a factor on which the success depends to a very large extent. The men selected must be qualified for the work, and they must also have the special qualifications required to meet polar conditions. They must be able to live together in harmony for a long period without outside communication, and it must be remembered that the men whose desires lead them to the untrodden paths of the world have generally marked individuality.

The hut that Shackleton and his men built during the Nimrod expedition is still standing in Antarctica. In the background is Mount Erebus, named after one of the ships of an earlier Antarctic explorer, James Ross.

The voyage south to Antarctica was not an easy one. A. L. A. MacKintosh, an officer aboard the *Nimrod*, wrote on January 3: "A truly miserable day and night: everything upside down, nearly everyone seasick. We exchanged signals with the *Koonya* occasionally–this afternoon, she inquired how our passengers were faring. We replied and told her that there were twenty seasick, but all cheerful."

The *Koonya* and *Nimrod* made their way through clusters of icebergs. It was slow going, because collision with an iceberg could prove disastrous.

On January 16, the *Nimrod* entered the Ross Sea, inching its way through cracks in the packed ice. Shackleton wanted to make camp at McMurdo Sound, but the ice was too heavy for the ship to pass through. On January 28, still 20 miles from what the men would call "Hut Point," the voyage of the *Nimrod* ended. The men unloaded their equipment and supplies and the *Nimrod* returned to New Zealand. Sleds and sled dogs had been brought, as well as some Siberian ponies—tough horses used to the freezing temperatures of northern Russia. Shackleton had also brought an automobile, to use for short trips away from the camp.

Over the next few months, the men did some exploring and scientific work. One of the early accomplishments of the mission was their ascent of the 3,795-foot Mount Erebus. "We were all busy, and there was little cause for us to find the time hanging heavy on our hands; the winter months sped by," wrote Shackleton.

On October 29, 1908, Shackleton set out for the Pole, accompanied by J. B. Adams, a meteorologist;

Dr. Eric Marshall, a physician who also served as the mission's mapmaker; and Frank Wild, who had been put in charge of the provisions.

The group encountered problems from the start. Adams was injured when he was kicked by one of the Siberian ponies. Later, he grew ill from a toothache, and Marshall had to pull the tooth. The skies were often cloudy, which meant the ledges, *crevasses*, mounds, and gullies cast no shadows. Without shadows, the men could not see dangerous obstructions in the flat, icy plains. Wild, Adams, and Marshall each had to be rescued from falls into crevasses.

Also, the explorers had not brought enough food. As a result, they had to cut back on meals. That meant constant hunger for the men and animals. Later, they would kill one of the ponies for its meat. Despite this, Shackleton was confident. He wrote: "Difficulties are just things to overcome."

On November 29 the explorers passed the point where Scott's party had stopped six years before. Shackleton and his men had now gone further south than any previous expedition. By mid-December, they were still 250 miles from the Pole. Unfortunately, within days, the weather became so severe that they were able to travel only four miles a day.

In 1908 Shackleton was just 97 miles from the South Pole—the closest any explorer had yet come to the Pole— when he planted a British flag, then turned back.

"I cannot think of failure yet," wrote Shackleton. "I must look at the matter sensibly and consider the lives of those men who are with me. Man can only do his best."

By January 9, a severe blizzard had kept them huddled in their tents for two days. Shackleton, Adams, Marshall, and Wild left their tents, carrying a camera and a Union Jack—the British flag. They planted the flag, took a photograph, and recorded their position.

They were 97 miles from the South Pole.

And then they turned for home.

Shackleton's ice-covered ship, the Endurance, *is trapped in ice. When the wooden ship was crushed, sinking on November 15, 1915, the first priority of Shackleton's mission changed from exploration to survival.*

Endurance 5

ollowing the *Nimrod* mission, Shackleton returned to England, where the king and queen awarded him a knighthood. He would now be Sir Ernest Shackleton.

Meanwhile, two other missions headed for the South Pole. One was led by Robert Falcon Scott, the other by Roald Amundsen, a Norwegian. Amundsen would win the race. On December 14, 1911, Amundsen reached the South Pole, where he raised the flag of Norway. Scott's team arrived just over a month later. Amundsen lived to explore other lands, but Scott died in Antarctica. On the way back from the Pole, Scott and four members of his expedition died of starvation and exposure. Scott's body was found just 11 miles from his base camp.

Despite the success of Scott's and Amundsen's quests for the pole, Shackleton still believed there was a goal to accomplish in Antarctica. He wrote: "After the conquest of the South Pole by Amundsen who, by a narrow margin of days only, was in advance of the British Expedition under Scott, there remained but one great main object of Antarctic journeyings–the crossing of the South Polar continent from sea to sea."

As with most old families in Great Britain, the

Before reaching the South Pole, Roald Amundsen had already won fame as the first explorer to sail through the Arctic Ocean above North America– the fabled Northwest Passage, which explorers had sought since the time of Columbus. Amundsen would go on to traverse the

Northeast Passage above Asia, and become the first man to fly across the Arctic Circle.

Shackletons had a ***coat of arms***–an emblem that contains symbols that represent achievements in the family history. Inscribed into the Shackleton coat of arms is the Latin expression *Fortitudine Vincimus.* In English, this means, "By endurance, we conquer."

Certainly, Edward Shackleton intended to live up to that motto. Twice he had been denied the opportunity to be among the first men to stand at the South Pole. In 1914, he would make his third trip to Antarctica.

He proposed an 1,800-mile march across the continent, starting out at the Weddell Sea on the Atlantic Ocean, crossing Antarctica through the South Pole, and completing the mission near McMurdo Sound on the Pacific side.

By early December in 1914, Shackleton and his fellow explorers were aboard the ship *Endurance,* making their way through heavy ice in the Weddell Sea. The ship could barely inch along; often, the *Endurance* would be delayed several days until the ice shifted and the vessel could break free.

On January 19, 1915, the *Endurance* could not continue. The ship was completely stuck in ice. The expedition's only hope was for the ice entrapping the ship to drift out to the warmer sea, where the

Endurance would be able to break free. For months, Shackleton and the others waited. But Shackleton couldn't help noticing that, instead of their ice prison drifting toward warmer waters, more ice was moving toward the ship. "The ice is rafting to a height of ten or fifteen feet in places," he wrote. "The opposing ice floes are moving against one another at the rate of about 200 yards per hour. The noise resembles the roar of heavy, distant surf. Standing on the stirring ice, one can imagine it is disturbed by the breathing and tossing of a mighty giant below."

Nine months after the *Endurance* became stuck, the ship was crushed by the shifting ice. For weeks, pressure against the hull had been building. Before the *Endurance* sank on October 27, the men unloaded food, supplies, equipment, and three lifeboats onto the ice.

Shackleton and the others were able to make camp atop a massive ice floe. They remained there for the next several months, while this ice drifted west for several hundred miles. But on April 9, 1916, with the ice floe under them disintegrating in the Weddell Sea, the men had to face the prospect of escaping from Antarctica in the tiny, open lifeboats. The boats—the *James Caird*, *Stancomb Wills*, and

Shackleton's sled dogs watch as the Endurance *sinks slowly into the frigid waters of the Weddell Sea.*

Dudley Docker–were each equipped with a small mast and sail as well as oars. However, there was no shelter aboard. The voyage would have to be made with no protection from the elements.

The men's first goal was Elephant Island, a small stretch of land in the Weddell Sea. They made it to the island on April 15 and camped there for nine days. During this time, Shackleton concluded that the only hope for rescue was to reach the island of South Georgia, 800 miles distant. Shackleton took five men with him on the journey in the *James Caird*, considered the sturdiest and most **seaworthy** of the three boats. The crew included Frank Worsley, captain of the *Endurance*; three sailors from the *Endurance*, Tom Crean, John Vincent, and Tim McCarthy; and Harry McNeish, the ship's carpenter.

The others stayed behind on Elephant Island to await a rescue party that Shackleton would send once he reached safety. Shackleton left Frank Wild, his second-in-command, in charge of the 22 men remaining on the island. The men on Elephant Island faced weeks or possibly months of growing darkness with only seals and penguins to supplement their shrinking food supplies.

On April 24, 1916, the *James Caird* set sail for South Georgia, in what would become one of the greatest small-boat voyages in history.

On May 10–the 16th day of the voyage of the *James Caird*–Shackleton guided the tiny lifeboat onto the rocky shore of South Georgia. The journey of the *James Caird* was over, but the men still had to make their way across the rugged South Georgia landscape to reach the whaling station. They had come ashore on King Haakon Bay; the Norwegian whaling station at Stromness Bay was located on the island's north coast. They would have to undertake a treacherous 17-mile march over a mountain range that divided South Georgia.

Shackleton decided to leave McNeish and Vincent behind at King Haakon Bay; the two men were too weak to make the trip. McCarthy was left behind as well to care for the injured men.

After resting for five days, Shackleton, Crean, and Worsley set out to cross the South Georgia mountains. For the next 36 hours, they climbed icy slopes, some as high as 4,500 feet. They continued to march throughout the night; a full moon was out, which provided light for the climb. Just before seven o'clock in the morning on May 16, the three men were making their way through some rock formations when Shackleton thought he heard the sound of a steam whistle. It was the wake-up call for whalers at Stromness Bay. They made their way to the wharf of the whaling station, where they

On reaching the top of one ice-covered peak in South Georgia, Shackleton told his companions, Tom Crean and Frank Worsley, "Let's slide." Seated on a coiled rope, the three men went "shooting down the side of an almost precipitous mountain at nearly a mile a minute," Worsley later wrote. Laughing and exhilarated when they reached the bottom, the adventurers shook hands, then continued their 36-hour journey.

encountered a man working on the docks. "Who are you?" the man asked.

"We have lost our ship and come over the island," Shackleton answered.

The man could hardly believe them.

"You have come over the island?" he said in a tone of disbelief.

At the whaling station, the exhausted men were given food and baths, and they told their story. The whalers quickly launched rescue missions. Worsley went aboard a ship bound for King Haakon Bay to rescue McNeish, Vincent, and McCarthy. Two days later, Shackleton rode aboard the Norwegian whaling ship *Southern Sky* to rescue the men waiting on Elephant Island. But the *Southern Sky* had to turn back because the ice was too thick. Not until August 30, with Shackleton aboard the Chilean steamship *Yelcho*, were the men rescued.

As a landing boat from the *Yelcho* approached the Elephant Island coast, Shackleton called out to Frank Wild: "Are you all well?"

Wild called back, "All safe, all well!"

Amazingly, not a single man who had accompanied Shackleton aboard the *Endurance* died during the long ordeal.

Final

Expedition

Sir Ernest Shackleton waves farewell as his ship, the Quest, *sets out for the Antarctic in September 1921. This expedition would turn out to be Shackleton's last; he died on January 5, 1922, and was buried on South Georgia Island.*

6

ollowing the rescue of the men on Elephant Island, Shackleton returned to England in May 1917 to find his country in the midst of World War I. At 42, Shackleton was too old to fight on the front lines. Instead, he headed for South America, where he served in the British government's *propaganda* office. His job was to convince Argentina to enter the war on the side of the Allies. He met with little success. Later, he traveled to

Norway to take over a weather station that had been abandoned by the Germans.

The station was on the Norwegian island of Spitsbergen above the Arctic Circle. It would be the first time that this veteran of three Antarctic adventures would have a chance to visit the opposite side of the planet. But while en route to Spitsbergen, during a stay in the Norwegian city of Tromsø, Shackleton suddenly fell ill. He returned to England, unaware that his illness had been caused by a weakening heart.

After the war, Shackleton found few people interested in the heroic voyage of the *James Caird*. In keeping with the grim toll World War I had exacted from Britain, most people seemed more interested in the tragic story of Scott's death in Antarctica. By 1920, Shackleton, bored with his life, was drinking heavily, smoking frequently, eating too much, and aching for more adventure. He started talking to friends about one more exploration. One of the men he approached was John Quiller Rowett, who had gone to school with Shackleton. He was now wealthy and interested in financing scientific ***endeavors***. He agreed to put up the money for another Antarctic expedition.

Actually, the goals of this trip were not very ambitious. Shackleton had no desire left for a prolonged trek across the continent. This time, most of the exploring would be done aboard ship, as Shackleton proposed a *circumnavigation* of the Antarctic continent. He also intended to make side trips to sub-Antarctic islands. For example, Shackleton thought he could find pirate treasure that was supposedly buried on South Trinidad Island in the South Atlantic.

Shackleton obtained an old Norwegian whaling ship, renamed her the *Quest*, and on September 17, 1921, shoved off for Antarctica. In late December, the *Quest* was making its way down the Brazilian coast when Shackleton became gravely ill. He had probably suffered a heart attack. Despite this, Shackleton refused to turn back.

On January 4, 1922, the *Quest* anchored in South Georgia's Stromness Bay. Shackleton was greeted by many of the Norwegian whalers who had helped rescue the explorers from the *Endurance* some six years before. Shackleton went ashore to spend the night with his old friends.

Early the next morning, Alexander Macklin, the doctor traveling aboard the *Quest*, was summoned to

Shackleton's grave on South Georgia. In recent years, Shackleton's adventures have been retold in many new books and films.

Shackleton's room. He found Shackleton stricken with another heart attack.

Macklin told Shackleton that after the voyage to Antarctica, he would do well to stop exploring and settle down to a quiet life in England. "You're always wanting me to give up things," Shackleton complained. "What is it I ought to give up?" A few minutes later, Sir Ernest Shackleton was dead.

When Emily Shackleton was told that her husband had died, she asked that he be buried on South Georgia. She knew he would want to remain in the "mysterious south" that he had loved so passionately.

At the time of his death, Ernest Shackleton's accomplishments had been overshadowed by those of the ill-fated Robert Scott. But recently there has been a renewed interest in Shackleton and his expeditions, resulting in new exhibits and books about the explorer as well as a PBS/Nova-sponsored TV ***documentary film*** and an IMAX film, *Shackleton's Antarctic Adventure.* This contemporary interest in Shackleton's heroic journey is not surprising. Nearly 100 years later, the escape from the *Endurance* to South Georgia, as well as the 17-mile march over the island's mountains, remains one of history's most remarkable and successful battles waged by man against the elements.

Chronology

1774 English Explorer James Cook is first to sail through Antarctic waters.

1874 Ernest Henry Shackleton is born on February 15 in County Kildare, Ireland.

1890 Joins the crew of the full rigger *Hoghton Tower*.

1899 On February 18, Norwegian Karsten Borchgrevink becomes the first to set foot on the Antarctic continent.

1901 Shackleton sails for Antarctica August 6, aboard the ship *Discovery* in an expedition led by Robert Falcon Scott.

1902 After marching across the Antarctic continent with Scott, comes within 480 miles of the South Pole on December 31.

1904 Marries Emily Dorman on April 9.

1908 Aboard the *Nimrod,* arrives back in Antarctica on January 28, leading his own expedition.

1909 Marches to within 97 miles of the South Pole before turning back on January 9.

1911 Norwegian Roald Amundsen reaches the South Pole on December 14.

1912 Scott reaches the South Pole on January 17. He and his men are trapped in a blizzard and die from exposure and starvation while returning to their base camp.

1915 On January 19, Shackleton returns to Antarctica a third time; his ship *Endurance* becomes mired in ice, and is crushed October 27.

1916 On April 15, sails to Elephant Island with crew from *Endurance* aboard three lifeboats; on April 24, sets out for South Georgia in the open lifeboat *James Caird* with five others, arriving May 10.

1921 Travels aboard the *Quest* on his fourth trip to Antarctica in September.

1922 Dies January 5 at the whaling station at Stromness Bay, South Georgia.

2001 IMAX film about Shackleton's *Endurance* expedition and the voyage of the *James Caird,* entitled *Shackleton's Antarctic Adventure,* is released in February.

Glossary

axis–a straight line around which a planet rotates.

capsize–to cause to overturn.

circumnavigation–sailing completely around a geographical feature.

coat of arms–a symbolic emblem that depicts a persons' or family's heritage or accomplishments.

crevasse–a deep crack in a glacier or land formation.

documentary film–a movie that takes a factual and objective look at its subject.

endeavor–an effort directed toward a certain goal.

equator–the imaginary line around the middle of the Earth.

expedition–a group of people making a journey for a specific purpose, such as discovery or exploration.

iceberg–a large block of ice floating in the ocean.

insulation–a material that traps heat so it can't escape.

latitude–the imaginary horizontal lines mapmakers use to locate places on the Earth.

magnetism–a force that attracts objects, usually seen in magnets and iron.

merchant marine–a country's commercial ships.

peninsula–a piece of land surrounded by water on three sides.

potable–safe to drink.

propaganda–ideas, facts, or rumors spread to help change public opinion about a cause or group of people.

reef–hard underwater ridges of rocks and coral that form near shorelines.

scurvy–a disease caused by lack of vitamin C, which was
common on long journeys where fresh food, especially
fruits and vegetables, were not available. Its symptoms
include spongy gums and loose teeth, soreness in the
arm and leg joints, and bleeding into the skin and
mucous membranes.

seaworthy–safe for a sea voyage.

snow blindness–a painful condition caused by exposure of the
eyes to ultraviolet rays reflected from snow or ice.

tiller–a lever used to turn the rudder of a boat from side to side,
which in turn helps to steer the boat.

Further Reading

Alexander, Caroline. *The Endurance: Shackleton's Legendary Antarctic Expedition.* New York: Alfred A. Knopf, 1999.

Fogg, G. E., and David Smith. *The Explorations of Antarctica.* London: Cassell Publishers Limited, 1990.

Kimmel, Elizabeth Cody. *Ice Story: Shackleton's Lost Expedition.* New York: Clarion Books, 1999.

Lansing, Alfred. *Endurance: Shackleton's Incredible Voyage.* New York: Carroll and Graf, 1999.

Neider, Charles. *Antarctica.* New York: Random House, 1972.

Shackleton, Ernest. *South!* New York: Carroll and Graf, 1998.

–––. *The Heart of the Antarctic: Being the Story of the British Antarctic Expedition, 1907-1909.* New York: Carroll and Graf, 1999.

Worsley, F. A. *Shackleton's Boat Journey.* New York: W. W. Norton and Company Inc., 1977.

Picture Credits

HAL MARCOVITZ is a reporter for the *Allentown (Pa.) Morning Call.* His work for Chelsea House includes biographies of explorers Francisco Vazquez de Coronado, John C. Frémont, and Marco Polo; the Indian guide Sacagawea; and the Apollo astronauts. He lives in Chalfont, Pennsylvania, with his wife, Gail, and daughters, Ashley and Michelle.